Let's create more art together!

After the positive response to my first book "No Shenanigans! Mixed Media Painting", I just couldn't wait to bring you more colour, more mixed media magic and more SUNSHINE!

Painting is the most delightful thing to do in life (me, biased?!) and as I play and experiment every day in my colourful studio, my collection of paintings and ideas keeps on growing!

One sunny winter morning after a busy art journaling session, I gave up on trying to scrub off the lovely teal and magenta paint off my hands and decided to enjoy the sunshine instead...

I grabbed my art journals, sat on the grass still cool from the early morning and started slowly flicking through the slightly crackly pages... I paid attention to the details on each page rather than the finished spreads, noticing the delicious colour combinations, the bumpy texture of the paint, the intricate details from my hand carved stamps and stencils...
Each page is like a chapter in my life and there is a lot of happiness in these journals!
I then walked back to my studio and looked at the paintings hanging on the walls, once again paying attention to the details rather than the finished designs.
Finally, I thought to myself...

How can all this arty goodness be used to create even more art?
How can I make my art go further and share it in a way that is useful and inspiring?

And then a lightbulb went on!!!
It is then with great excitement and joy in my heart that I decided to put together a huge collection of 98 mixed media backgrounds, taken from my art journals and canvas paintings, in the hope they will make your head buzz with exciting ideas!

Please use the pages of this book in any way you like to start new creative adventures or, simply use this book as your own, already-started art journal by writing, doodling and painting directly on the pages... Use it and re-use it, and remember ,the only rule is to **create more art!!**

With love and sunshine, always... *Mimi*

Aqua Blue

PUBLISHING

Aqua Blue Publishing
A.B.N. 642 148 89 370
aquabluepublishing.com

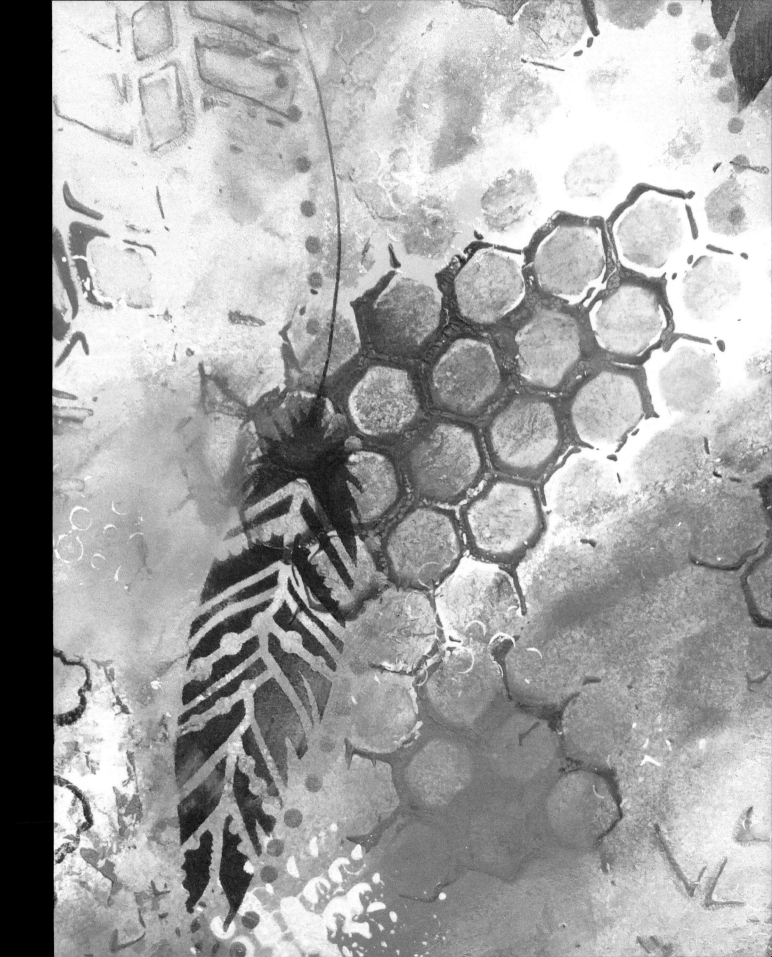

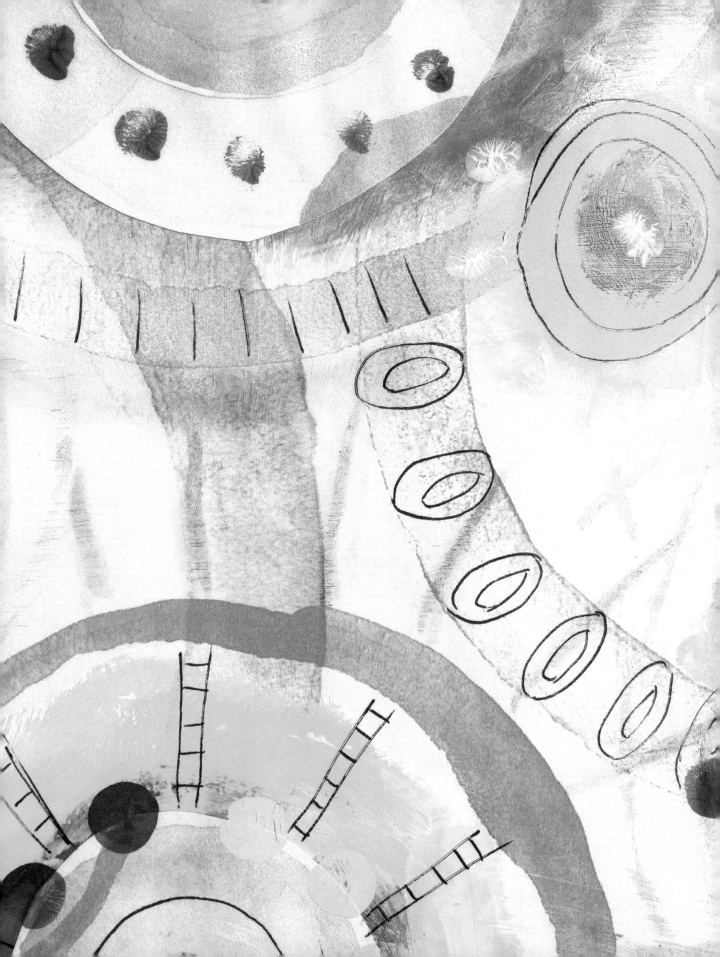

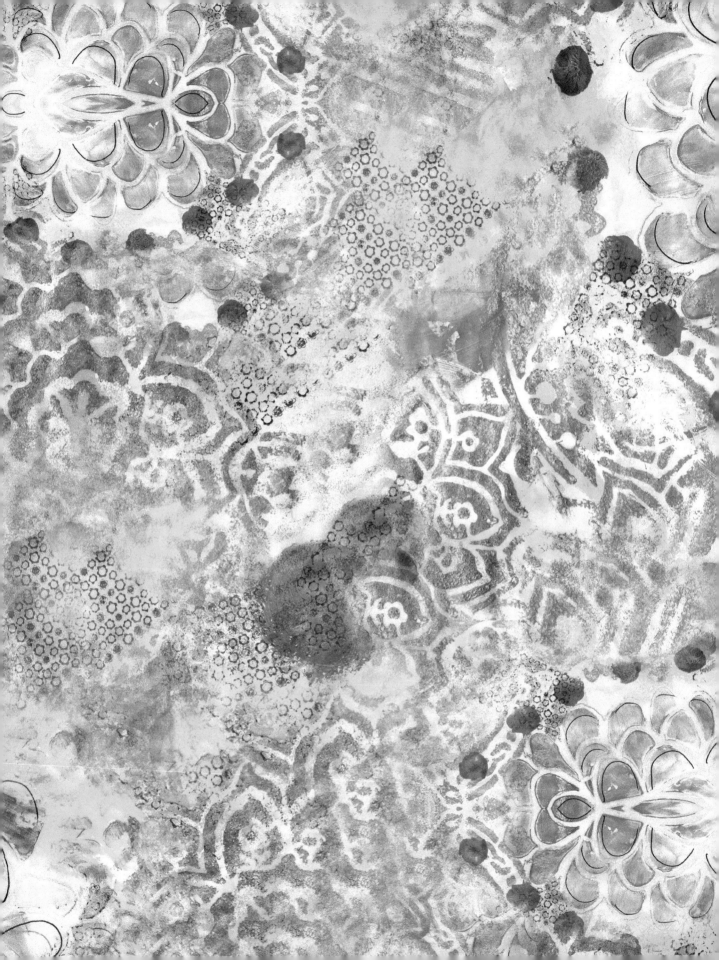

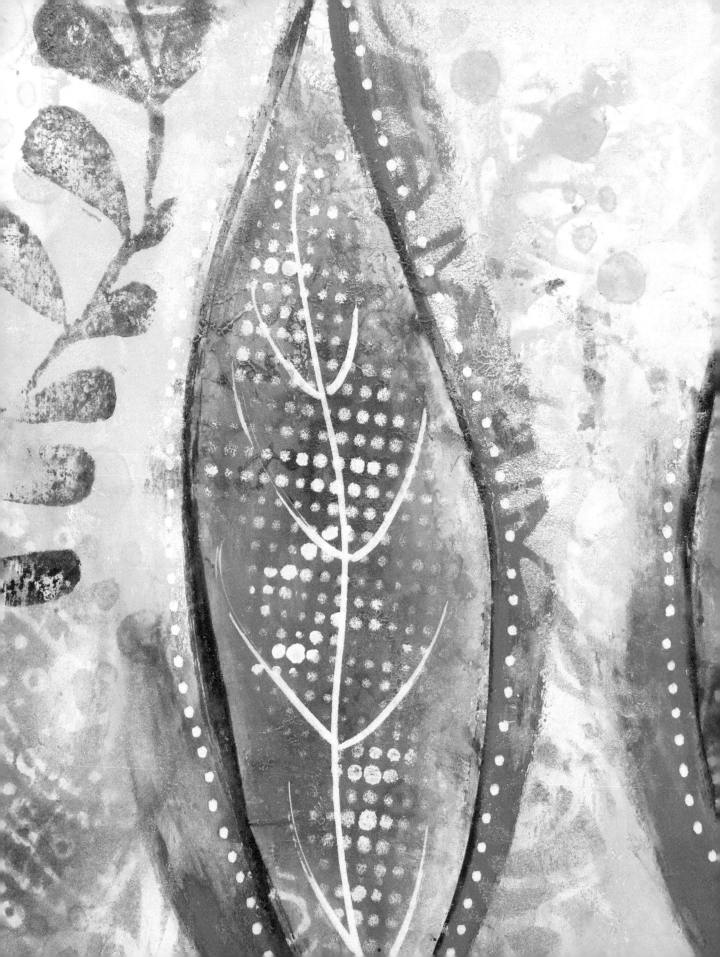

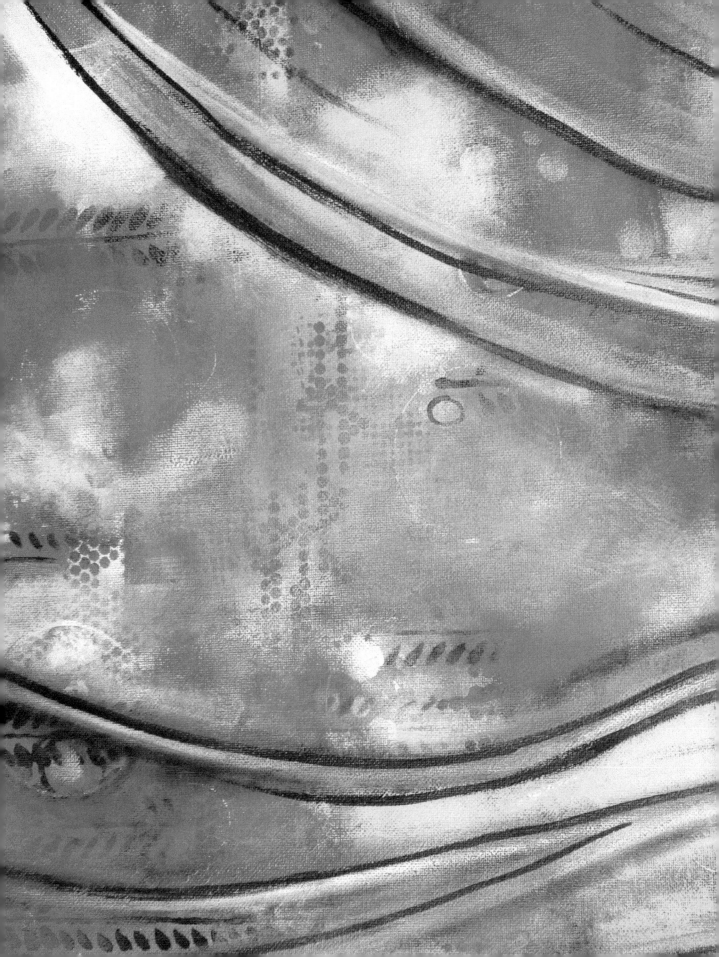

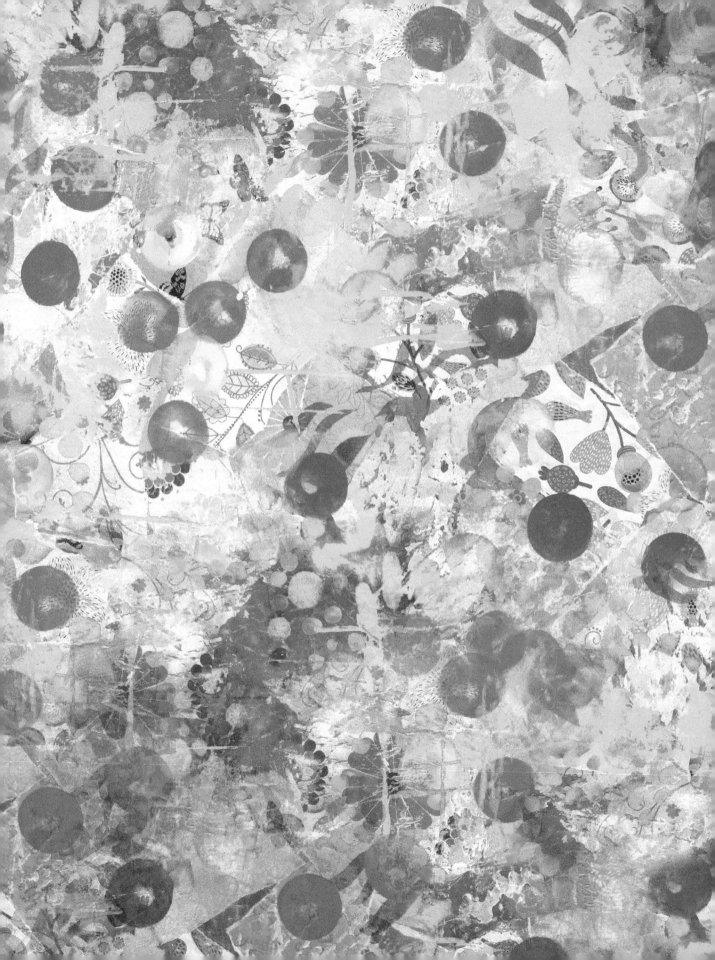

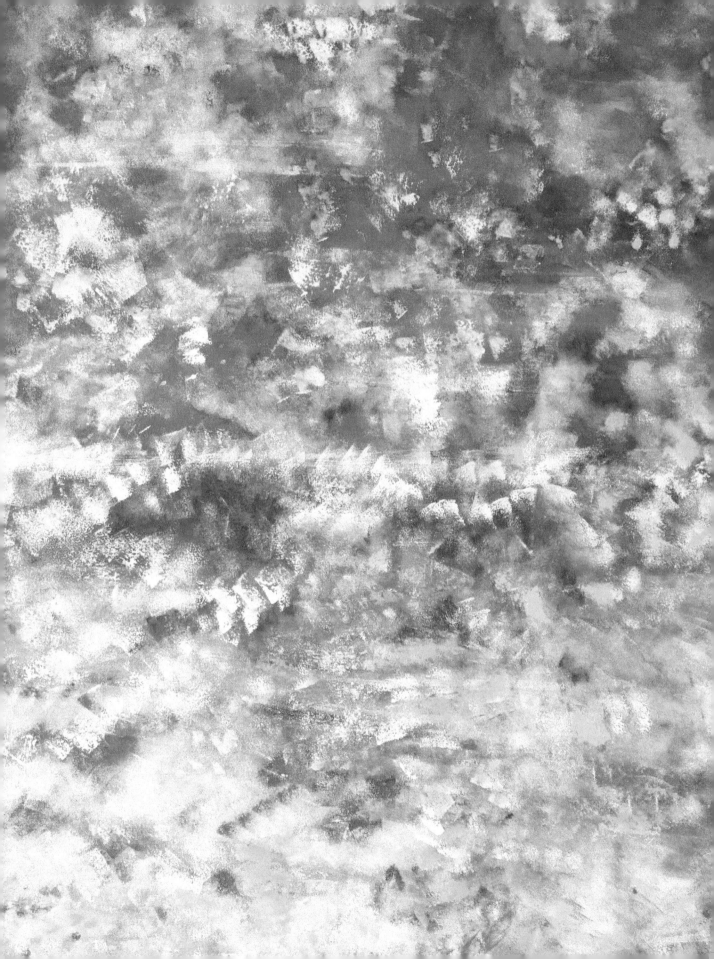

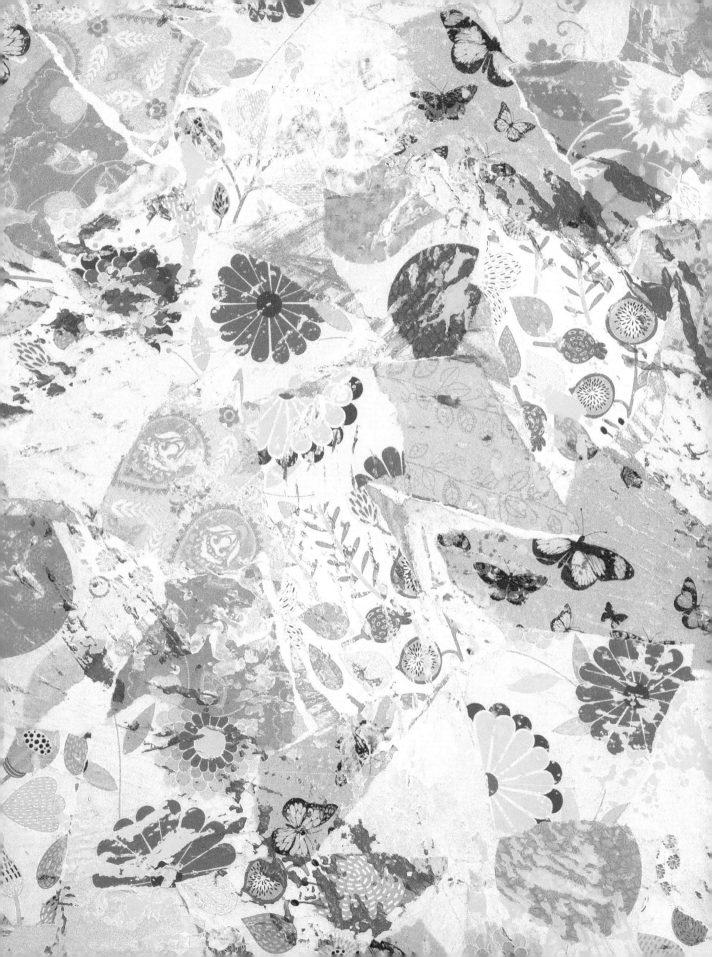

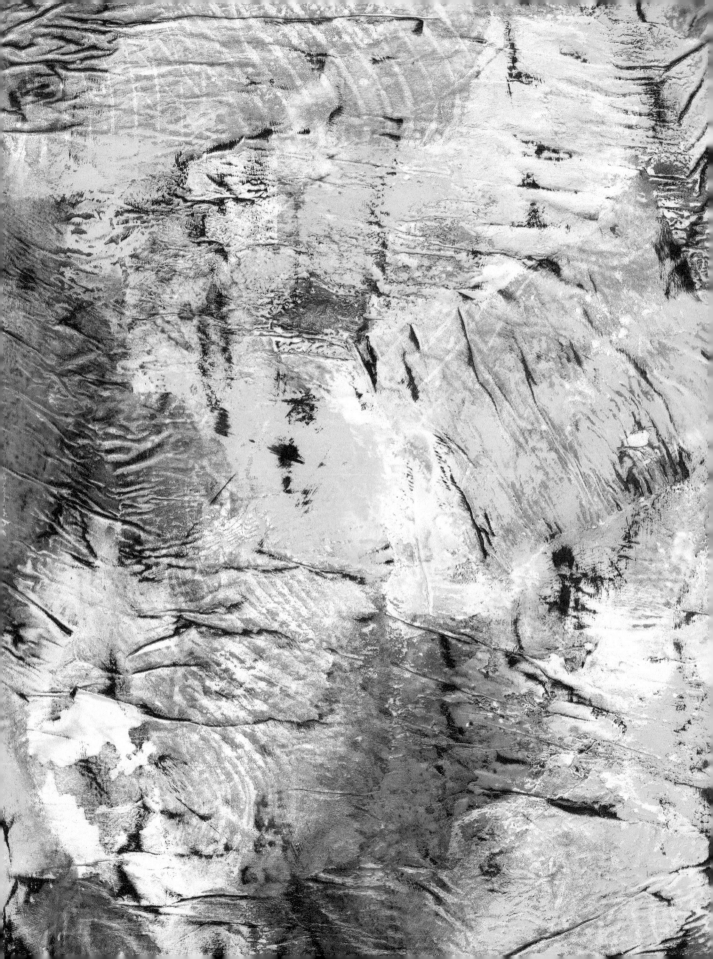

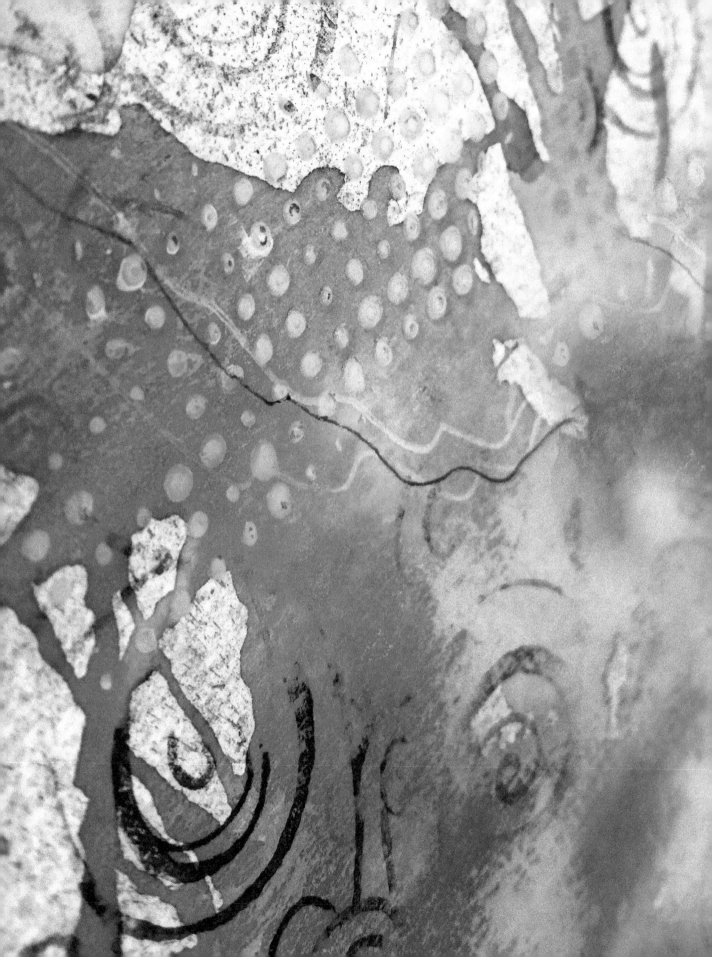

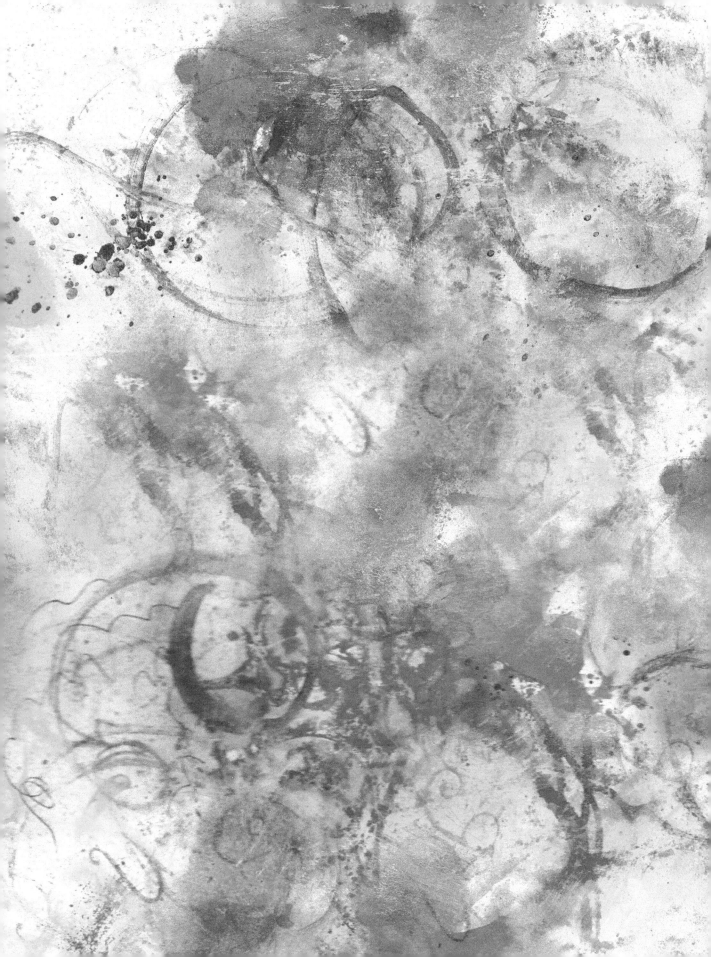

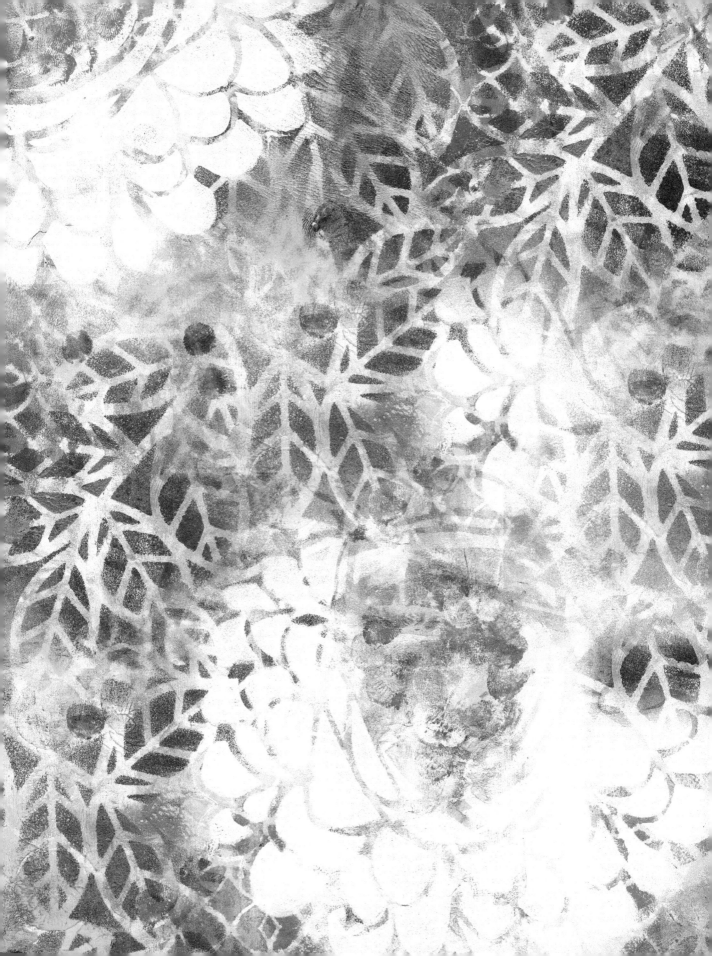

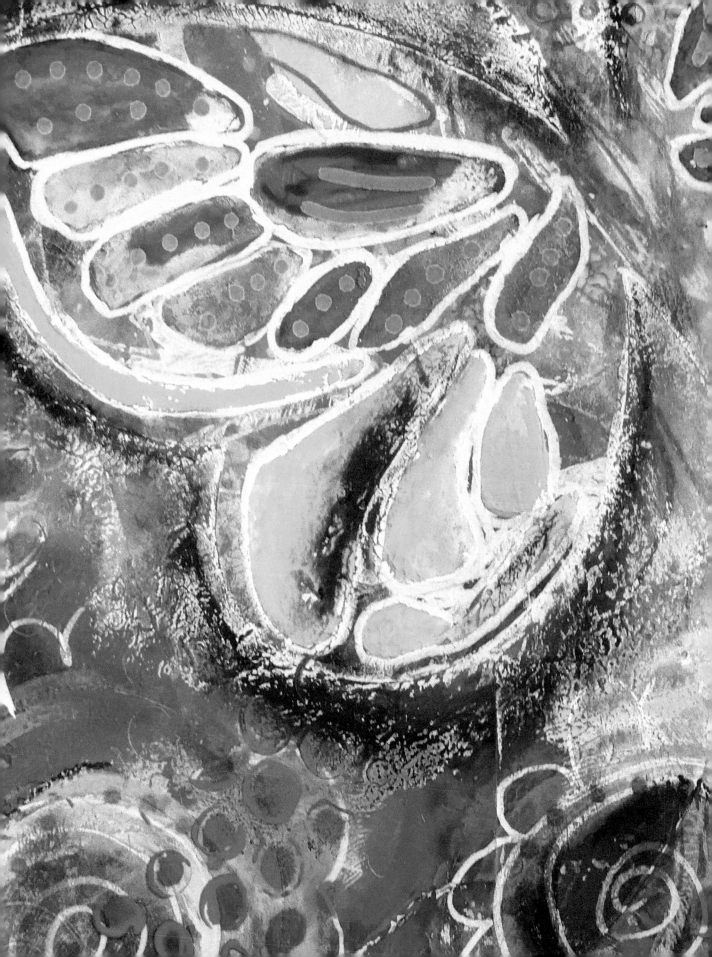

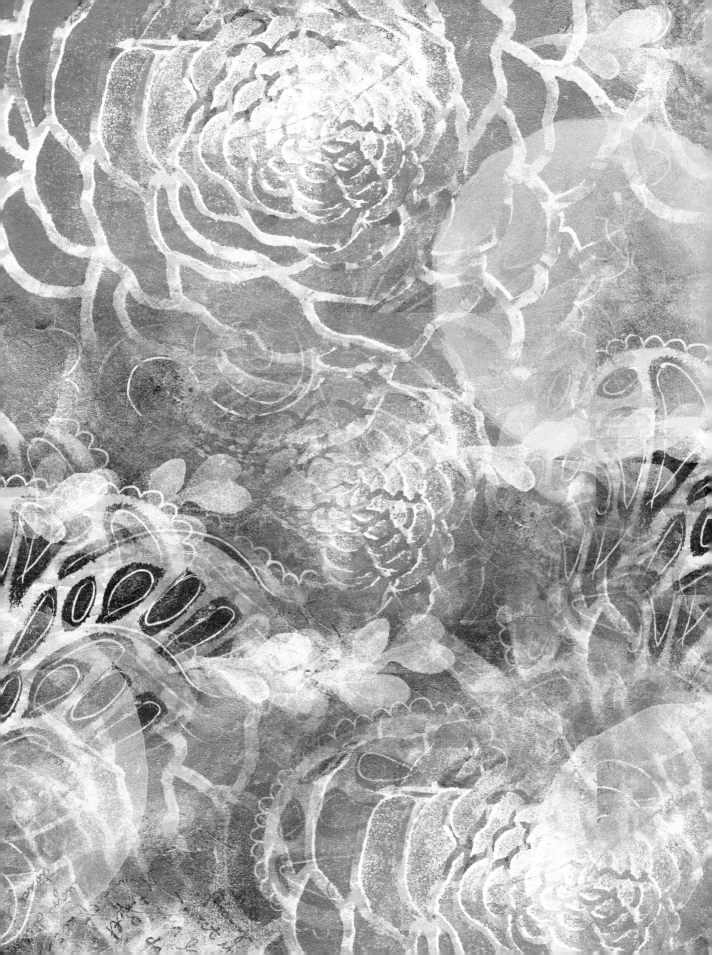

Questions, Comments?

The Mixed Media Tribe

If you would like to ask me a question about this book, share photos of the work you created from it and get support from other like-minded artists then... Please join my private Facebook group!

https://www.facebook.com/groups/mixedmediatribe

Find me on social media!

Facebook
For work in progress, new paintings and videos, new posts and exhibitions, find me on Facebook: *facebook.com/mimibondiart*

Instagram
For (almost) daily posts on highly talented & inspiring artists, photos of my work in progress, art journal pages and a few snippets from my personal life, find me on Instagram: *instagram.com/mimibondi*

YouTube
For free mixed media tutorials, travel vlogs and giveaways, find me on YouTube: *youtube.com/mimibondi*

Pinterest
An amazing social media platform where I collect TONS of ideas and arty inspiration on various art boards such as 'For the Love of Mixed Media', 'The Beauty of Abstract Art', 'Turquoise Addict, 'Whimsical Girls', 'Inspiring Words' and many more! Find me on Pinterest: *pinterest.com/mimibondi*

Stay in touch now, will you?

Sunshine Newsletter

Now that we have found each other, I hope we can stay connected!

**My Sunshine Newsletter is all about positivity and the BEST
way to keep up with all the good stuff in one central place:**

• Be the first to know about new books and online workshops

Who knows what I have in store for you lovely artists! But when new goodies are
cooking, I will be sharing them with you in my newsletter and give you priority access!

• Find out about new paintings I create

I will share new artworks with you and hopefully provide you with a little inspiration!

• Think positive, Be Positive, Paint Positive

I am all about positivity and love to find, write and share articles and tools that can
make a positive impact in your life... and make you a better artist!

• Free art journal video tutorials

If you want to learn new techniques and follow me along while I chat, play and
experiment in my art journal, you will find video links to my tutorials in the newsletter!

• Inspiring talented artists

Whenever I come across artists who blow my mind and who I think you will also enjoy,
I write a post about them and share a link to their website so you too can be amazed
and inspired!

**My Sunshine Newsletter comes out every week and if you
are not receiving it yet, visit this page now before you forget!**

mimibondi.com/newsletter

Learn mixed media with highly detailed tutorials from start to finish!

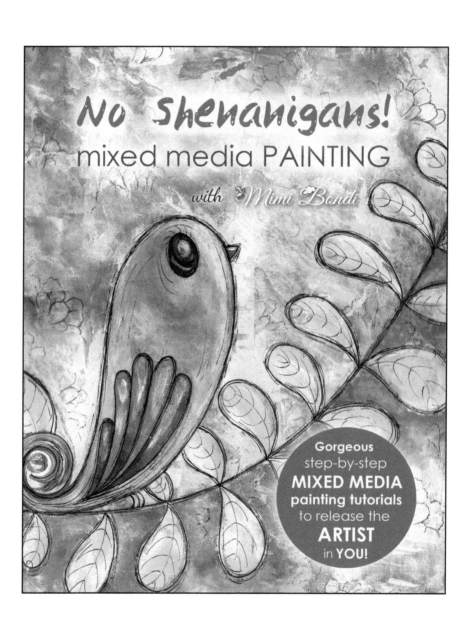

No Shenanigans!
mixed media PAINTING

with *Mimi Bondi*

Gorgeous
step-by-step
MIXED MEDIA
painting tutorials
to release the
ARTIST
in **YOU!**

Lightning Source UK Ltd.
Milton Keynes UK
UKHW050854190419
341303UK00001B/9/P